EACH LUMINOUS THING

ALSO BY STACIE CASSARINO

NONFICTION

Culinary Poetics and Edible Images in Twentieth-Century American Literature (2018)

POETRY

Zero at the Bone (2009)

Each Luminous Thing

POEMS

Stacie Cassarino

A Karen & Michael Braziller Book
Persea Books / New York

Persea Books, Inc.
90 Broad Street
New York, New York 10004

Library of Congress Cataloging-in-Publication Data

Names: Cassarino, Stacie, author.
Title: Each luminous thing : poems / Stacie Cassarino.
Description: First edition. | New York : Persea Books, [2023] | "A Karen & Michael
    Braziller Book." | Summary: "Winner of the 2022 Lexi Rudnitsky Editor's Choice
    Award"—Provided by publisher.
Identifiers: LCCN 2023021732 | ISBN 9780892556014 (paperback)
Subjects: LCGFT: Poetry.
Classification: LCC PS3603.A86823 E23 2023 | DDC 811/.6—dc23/eng/20230522
LC record available at https://lccn.loc.gov/2023021732

Book design and composition by Rita Lascaro
Typeset in Charter
Manufactured in the United States of America. Printed on acid-free paper.

for Sofia, Lucia, & Stella

ACKNOWLEDGMENTS

Thank you to my wonderful editor, Gabe Fried, whose eye on these poems lifted them up and out into the world, and to everyone at Persea Books for their care with the details.

Thanks to the editors of the following publications in which some of these poems first appeared: *Bennington Review*, *The Cortland Review*, *The Greensboro Review*, *Kenyon Review*, *Poetry Northwest*, *Poetry Daily*, and *Willow Springs*.

Thanks to Isabelle Menin for sharing her stunning art for my cover.

I'm grateful to all the friends who've shared in the making of this book: readers of my work, mothers sharing the juggle, artists walking alongside me, caretakers of my children, especially Dima Ayoub, Ann Cronin, Erin Davis, Cheryl Faraone, Katie Flagg, Deb Evans, Barbara Ganley, Geoffrey Gevalt, Sarah Hansen, Kathy Harding, Jaden Hill, Laurel Jenkins, Sarah Lagrotteria, Michelle Leftheris, Brett Millier, Lana Povitz, Taly Ravid, Bill Roper, Patty Ross, Ali Shapiro, and many others. Thanks to my students whose poems teach me. I couldn't have written this book without the support of my parents, essential in all ways. Thanks to my whole family for the deepest love. Thanks to James Smith who made my journey possible. And for sources of luminosity at the core of this book: my three children, and the vibrant spirits of Matthew Power, Rose Cassarino, and Giustina D'Angelo Vignone, whose presence is in everything.

CONTENTS

I

II

III

IV

Often when I imagine you
Your wholeness cascades into many shapes.
You run like a herd of luminous deer
and I am dark, I am forest.
—RAINER MARIA RILKE

I

June Landscape with Child

The world is gone, I have to carry you.
   —PAUL CELAN

On the Charmlee bluffs nine months
since you were pronounced alive

I don't wake you, dream-
slumped in my pack, exposed

to the whole disentangled world before us,
phantom sea, soft lip of land

dense with sage scrub, the salted breath
of belonging to one another, the spool

of light unwound, such trust
in my body to hold yours

adrift, careening through cloud-fields,
I don't dare disturb the gentle-

limbed surrender, or turn back
to say *here is the life I made,*

each blooming thing coming into view
for us to praise.

If we follow the hand-drawn legend,
this is a world of primary nouns:

to meadow, to ocean, to ruins.
Tell me again there's no god,

or these instructions for beauty
are ancient as the oak grove we rise from

to reconcile self with place, self
with other, sleeping child

with abstract scenery, mother
with future—an elegy that begins:

*Joy is so easy to access
here*. It's all a blur,

a jumble of landmarks
transmuted to scars

remembered as home,
and none of us needs directions

for what comes next. East,
west, cliff, canyon, tinder bones

of the toppled ranch, and the striking
golden invasion of mustard stalks everywhere

we step—a year from now fire
will take all of this with it.

And what would it have looked like
when you opened your eyes for the first time,

lopsided, nameless, lustrous,
any one of those animals

who would not wait to be overcome,
to clutch anything that might combust,

saying *save me, save me, save me*.

The Bats This Summer

Every sundown we start out
as clear forms. I am the daughter
walking beside the mother and
I am the mother pulling the daughter
through the darkening world and
I am no one's wife.

By the time we return
home we've become ourselves
mere vanishings. This is how night
is made. A few stars if we're lucky,
and the bats that swoop so near
as if they detect my fear—
how foolish I must look, cowering
for no reason while they wrest
any living matter whole.

My daughter gazes up
for each luminous thing my mother
is willing to affirm. Later, no one
will hold my worries. Like everything
else in summer, we move in circles,
chased by the longing for more.
More birdsong. More mountain. More moon.
I am trying to love even the ugly things
of this world. I am sure
they're coming for me.

Malibu Before the Woolsey Fire

At Nicholas Pond in the seventh month
of your tenancy

I hardly notice the terrain,
gravelly, fissured, arterial,

the way it wants rain
and the rain wants a mouth

and the mouth wants something
to devour,

the creatural way you remind me
I am not alone,

every footstep kicking up dust,
the sky so blue   it hurts to look,

swaths of yellowing tarweed
where we expect nothing

but this, this—
the way you want to be born.

Eclipse of Dying Baby

I.
Days before you were born
I stood alone

on a side street, looking up
as the disk of the moon covered the sun.

Maybe it lasted seconds.
Maybe I felt the graze of your hand along a rib

in the tumble. I know something about darkness,
how it moves towards us

then away, the doctor with her faint voice saying:
eventually she will tire of breathing.

II.
First you will learn object permanence,
then you will learn to walk.

You will walk towards things
that disappear.

On the screen: two sick lungs,
each perfect bone of your spine.

There is no way for me
to stop your suffering.

III.
Is it grief that makes the whale
swim in a phalanx surrounding the dead,

all the while composing song;
that makes the elephant raise a foot

over each unmoving body
with silent inspection; that makes

the hollowed-out woman with no baby to hold
a mother?

Body Electric

Before I was a mother,
I would crawl along these crags,
all spunk and grace, no qualm.
But today, on the top
of Buck Mountain, pregnant
with twins, I don't let myself yearn
for the woman carrying my daughter
with the tenderness of a woman
who will eventually need me
too. From the valley, anyone might look
up to see *family*. Look how they've arrived
to take in the view. And maybe

I pretended, every part of me swelling
and flushed and laboring to get there,
each step tactical, a triumph. But
this wasn't a story I could live with.
And when the thunderclouds came so quickly
all I could think was how reckless
I had been, putting the one life I'd made
into another woman's hands, while
we rushed down the slope
of shale and sludge, the path surging
with rainwater, my daughter somewhere
behind me, I ran and I ran
counting the seconds between the flash
and the sound to equal the distance
it might take to get struck, knowing
the same body that was a conductor
could not also be a shelter;
knowing how rare it is
to not want to be touched by light.

Low Tide in Truro with My Mother

Although I know it is inaccurate
to attribute human emotions

to animals, when I see
the marred loon

while walking North along the beach
at low tide with my mother

who fills my daughter's bucket
with shells she calls *pretty*,

one of her wings hanging
there, useless,

how can I not call it sadness.
But this is where I go

wrong, to expect that something
of this world recognizes my own

stranding. Her red eyes
an utterance: *put me back*

together. So when my mother
warns me to keep a distance,

I remember the subheading, *violence*
of the loons, how we are wholly

interlopers, and leave her there.
A mile behind us, my first-

born sleeps in the shadow
of an umbrella tilted into the wind,

salt-lipped and aflush
with heat, knowing

I will return for her.
Miles ahead of us: the harbor

of wooden-hulled fishing vessels,
the breakwater, the dance club

where someone moved her body
against mine

before I knew what to do with it, *queer*
we cannot call it,

a word that makes me less
pretty. I couldn't have saved her

anyways, while my mother kept looking
for the ones we would treasure,

discarding the rest
with a sideways toss.

Mornings at the Lake

More echo than mirror, those mornings
at the lake with my daughter in the steady shadow
of the mountain, its rock-sunned cliffs closed
to protect peregrine falcons, and somewhere unseen
the Falls of Lana where bodies in their youth plummet—

not to die, but to live. I feel
the need to clarify this difference, how what appears
at first as one thing could be another. And look at her,
skipping her toes along the edge
where the cool shock of water meets land, unsure
if or how or when to plunge, such simple questions
of the self, zigzagging and squealing in delight,
or not questions at all, just the body's pure surrender
to water. I can't look away. It's everything
I want for her life, though at any point, she may need me
to save her. How will I know how to save her?

Summer has a way of stealing us back
in time. Of making us miss all the things
we never became. Her face, like the face of the girl
who went under when we were ten, just as I was learning
to swim towards her, bobbing at the surface, a splash
of laughter repeating across the stillness of air. Nothing
like drowning to wake the child from childhood.
It could have all been a dream, except when I dragged
her up to the sky, she remembered to breathe, and
it was me, I was the one sinking.

If the lake is the *earth's eye*, what does it see,
what do we want it to see, what story
will it tell about our failures? Around us, a dispersed pack
of fake coyotes ready to scare the geese, their beady eyes
watching us wade in the shallowest part.
I thought they were real. We all did.

Later, at her easel, she draws a square of blue
empty at its center. How pleasing, I think, a lake.
But then she tells me the story like it is: *I'm making a disaster*.
I look back and all I can hear is her voice calling me,
an echo from someplace she hasn't yet filled in.

Love Poem to August

I'm not sure if dusk falls
or rises when I look up
from watering the garden
towards my daughter's cry
inside the house. Outside,
bats looping in circles
that want to be seen, so nearly
striking every dimming object:
lamppost, lilac, elm, roofline,
face of the pregnant woman
watering the garden. If I were
to lose track of time, walk
until I forgot I was needed,
would that make me less necessary?

The body carries its weight
forward, unsteady. Pines blacken
against the blue-edged ledge
of this lonely evening
in which I am only a mother,
a mother only
until all goes quiet. Inside,
two forms beginning
to resemble daughters, already
learning to breathe. Outside,
the sky lowers its floating stars.
One body leans against another.
What I can still identify
hangs heavy then splits:
more than one thing in the dark—
creaturely, impatient—
waits for me.

Momentary Drowning at Silver Lake

The way in I know by heart:
past the falls, under power

lines, the silent rise,
then clearing

where I deliver you
into the source, so suddenly

for a moment
you are gone, erased

from the scene, (and who am I
without you?

and who would I have been?)
summer humming on,

the blue flash
of tandem damselflies,

while your arms paddle
along the bottom of the lake

for air, and the trees
close in around us.

Resurrections

Late summer one night
I carry my daughter

to the center of the dark
to watch heat lightning

flare up the spine of mountains.
It isn't real

yet I stand there
pretending for her, poised

for the beauty
that is only ours

to lose, which falsely returns,
each time dimmer.

Dead things don't talk, she told me once
on our knees at the garden

observing the worm I split
in half, each severed part still going

somewhere with the will of five hearts
while she described the bleeding

duck her teacher shoveled over
the fence: *it was very very dead*. No trace

of unpleasantness, her spade
tunneling the soil for more worms,

no mournful grasp
of the quiescence of a body.

Life's too short to agonize,
my friend wrote me before dying

of heat along the Nile.
We were going back and forth

about the unmade child
trembling in a dark room

saying only *monster*. Agony
is the body without a source

of water,
is the child I made

with the tube down her throat
in her chest, stomach, heel,

is the mother watching
the machine tell the new-

born heart
it can learn to live,

even with pain,
unable to touch her anywhere

without permission.
Today,

my daughter wakes me
from a dream

I am not ready to leave
to tell the story of how

her baby died in the night
then came alive (*don't worry*

she reassures me). And
who am I

to tell her we only get one life,
while refractions of sound

bent back toward the earth
trick us into seeing

each flash of light
for what it is,

nothing
like each first pleasure I came

to know, and its counter-force
sadness. Couldn't I just let her believe

in the everlasting bones
of this northern land,

in the godly love
that could keep bringing her back

to me, under this starless heaven,
held aloft and desperate not to die?

Northern June Amble

Hard to believe
we were ever cold—
the dark throne
of insects
reverently droning,
the heavy mantle
of warm air
tucking us deep
into valley, cradle
of godly sway
and animal sinew,
thrushes in their fluted
madness, adorning
this night-blooming palace
with merciful wonder.
This much
we know is ours,
then is taken.

Landscape in Mirror

There's a woman singing
a song, singing a song
I could love a woman
and the song is all I hear
driving North until the radio
goes static and no one's waiting
home for me at the end.
Aren't the mountains
a false security, scaled
for beauty, those three soft-
faced children a sight to witness.
And in the mirror the road's pure
diminishment. Every barn
is a picture of death. I know
what it looks like, the weight
of love or nothing
in the eyes of each animal
looking out through one mistaken hole
to see the world
cut in half, to think *that's romance.*
To think she's singing to me.
Later a field burned
and I almost turned
back for the woman to say never
stop singing, stop singing
and it will cost you my life.

Fireflies in Vermont

There we are at twilight
with the lurch of a wild animal

pacing under the thicket of our yard
for the first glimmer. I am not sure

how long I can carry her on my shoulders, soft-
bodied pulsing wonder,

but I don't remember
how to put her down. It is hard

to breathe in this air, stagnant and
sweltering, hushed—some things

I simply can't explain. *If you want
to catch one,*

you have to act like one. In-
destructible, vigilant, for-

giving of this momentary
radiance, a code

of too much wanting. Let me remind
you what I am here for. My breasts

are still sticky with milk, the babies
are finally asleep. Every-

thing that must be cared for
is in reach. If I was never one

for prayer,
why do I want to lower us to the earth

for a closer look? *The head*
is the sensory unit of the body.

The body is a lantern, fright-
fully exquisite. There was a girl

who took it apart, wing
by tender wing, and I was her

accomplice. We wore it well,
our fingers banded with shiny

stolen promises. It was magical.
Then we faded out.

How could I not have seen
our mistake in believing

the splendor could be ours?
How could I have wanted it

any other way?
Things were dying

while we were becoming alive.

II

A light here required a shadow there.
—VIRGINIA WOOLF

The Living at Dead Creek

We are either too early or too late
when we set out across the cattail marsh-
lands looking for the Snow geese
I have promised you. It is colder
than I prepared for, wind gusts
pushing our bodies from behind,
and the sun does not warm us
enough. There are days I categorize
as failed. When I lie down
on the floor among dinosaurs
and dolls, close my eyes and
pretend I'm dead, while my children
go about their lives, then
come pouncing on the raft
of my open heart. There I am
at forty-five, and all I can hear
is my daughter saying *I'm making you
alive.* And here we are, on a morning
when the clouds seem sketched against
the blue to save us from the idea
that it could be perfect, still-
flowering jewelweed along the banks,
an inflorescence of woolgrass and
bristly sedge, the creek wending
northward, all the way to the city,
flowing into the lake that separates us
from another country where I once danced
at the gay bar until morning
because I could. Migration,
I tell my daughter, is like going home.
It is a mystery to me, what comes
into focus for her, or does not.
The nature poem embellishes.
It takes the memory of this picture
and turns it outward so that we are
the only disruption in a world of hard

data: orange mountain lit
from within, godforsaken field and the
machinery of human defeat. Once,
this place was an ocean. Can't you feel it,
I want to ask her, but when I scan
the scene, she is already drifting.
How many other promises
won't I be able to keep? When
will she want to know where
she came from? Three geese take refuge.
There were supposed to be thousands
of them. They were supposed to put on
a show for us.

End of September

By morning the monarch's crippled wing slows
to a flutter as distant as touch.

The way I understand it, our bodies
all end this way.

What is still wanted is let go of—
strands of milkweed hitch to wind.

An orchard flares from the inside
out and we eat from it

like we were given something free.
There they are, the ones I've made:

daughter   daughter   daughter.

It is too early to know their pain.
My body for so long

was only a verb: to swallow.
Something in the air,

light off the eye that looks back
to see my hand clutching the ghost

of love. Someone stomping
on whatever life

there is left of it, and she is mine
as anything ever was—

over and over and over.

October Portrait at Blueberry Hill

Just past peak, the mountain
reminds me how late I have come again

to what matters. Out from
woods yellowed by time, our leafy stride

to the clearing where winter looks on,
I take note of the wind

pushing us along. It used to be
that I had only my own shadow,

but in this light I see your two legs
swinging, your two wing-like arms,

and you are ahead of me,
indecipherable from the splendor

of the world and what it keeps
giving. If it is true

that pain gets recorded elsewhere
in the body, I don't see it

for what it is. Around us
the hillside dormancy

of blueberry, ghost of summer
and the prayer I held

inside of me. Now,
I carry you outside of me

and narrate the silence in the trees,
unbearable and evanescent,

all that you will learn
that you will yearn for,

your two hands in the sky waving
for me to find you.

November at Ash Creek

No leeway of sails on the Sound,
not the wake of any moving thing

those mornings where I conceived
of you, how the sky

could remain above me,
allegiant and flat,

though it seemed to touch
down,

I followed the same ledge
of land imprecisely

knowing when you might appear.
Was it sorrow

or something else altogether
that came up in me

when I saw a child
up to her knees in the clam beds,

her father holding a rake,
a lone osprey watching over

from a stump in the reeds,
the tide pushing in.

Song For The Unborn Mother

In the birthing room, my sister torn
open, who once I held in the dark stories
of what we could not see, now a mother
before me, entering another world
while I stand on the margins of this one,
among numbered consolations, masks, hands
pulling for something alive, the Charles River
coiling in fluent green, *you can do this*,
though now I'm not sure whose voice
is speaking to whom, the mirror held
so she can see my face watching
what her wild body has made to let go of,
wrestle & blood-wreck, muscular clench, piss,
milk, sweat, estranged beauty; Out the window:
a scull recedes, we race blindingly, bravely,
inarticulate witnesses, a pulse, the whole
love-forging stench of it all.

After the Miscarriage

While my three daughters sleep,
I think of the fourth
and how hard her heart must have worked
while I went about each day, pumping
a threadless tire, pedaling to the end
of the littered pier just for the sensation
of being married to land, then dismounting.
I could have been any part of that scene:
the brooding angler, scraps
of gutted perch, the muscle
in the throat of the hovering gull.
Everything reeks. All I can hear
is the static of a.m. radio, broken
surf, broken Spanish, so many bodies
hurled by swells, an outcry, *reel it in*.
But who is there
to praise the retrieve? And who
will be gentle enough to release her?

LA Translations

Man is in love and loves what vanishes
—WILLIAM BUTLER YEATS

The lesson begins with division,
with words that trick us:
how to inflect the non-
finite, to forgive weakness
in the verb *to leave*, (a given
condition). At night
I hear my neighbor moaning
through the wall, and miss
the rain. It is raining
in New York, therefore it is you
I want to touch. Here, wires
drone and clack, boulevards
eventually end. We have power
then we don't. *I hate the palm trees,*
you say, *the bleak edifice, the distance
between us.* Walking down Sunset,
cars race home like neon promises,
a billboard flashes *life is beautiful,*
sells the boyish figure of *woman.*
A word can be borrowed,
though we are likely invaders.
With zero derivation, I put the roots
back to back. It is never enough.
I want to believe in home.
There is no grammatical future.
We are resplendent, we are partial,
then we are gone. I don't know
the word that brings us back.

Orca Elegy

They called it her *tour of grief*,
the path of the Orca carrying her dead calf

through the Salish Sea
for seventeen days while we, the human

audience, couldn't look away.
We understood

this kind of killer
might feel what only we could

designate in language
as mothers:

how she *won't let go*,
how she is *still holding on*,

and then the slow sinking
diminished body *finally dropped*

to nowhere. For seventeen days
after my daughter was born,

no one permitted me to carry her
home. In a room dark as water, I tracked

the science of her on a screen—pulse
oximetry, waveform, breathing

machine. Was it clinging or song:
How one body nourished

another, became a sudden source.
How the sky hung above,

a circular horizon,
then blood of a stranger

moved through her.
To float or to fall.

How I probed the seabed desperate
for lucent transmissions of hope.

Postpartum, Pacific Coast Time

Like any other mother, I break
the day into junctures:
up San Juan
down Santa Clara
across Electric Avenue—
Am I too late,
too methodical, a shadow
retracing the evacuation route?
What monsters surround
these fragile episodes of love?
Will I be undaunted?
Will she remember
pain, rocking her body
towards dream?
The wind is savory:
jasmine, salt of lemons.
Each palm tree leans protective.
It is me who knows abandon.
What summons the quiet
from lives otherwise
unnoticeable? Who flourishes
here? Looking west:
the surf in clear view, the woman
who keeps trying to stand
on water—a resemblance
to prayer. This is the way
home, past the sign
Never die alone, this
is how you let me be wild
beyond recognition.

The Life of Shadows

I. Erasure

To step into the shadow of this mountain
                              letting it untangle
              your breath
        To step into its shadow   to become a part
              of the mountain's life   not flat
                              but   voluminous

of   light
              of the bodies that secret   time
        that change   contours with   the season
              zones where
                  quiet   bodies
        sway
                      free   making

                              shelter

                  of the world
slipping out   of the palace to wander

                                        if only
                      To find oneself in the shadow
of a mountain   exposed to the private

        world that lies beneath it, to enter
                                        radiance

37

II. Restoration

The way I understand it,

when my daughter's dazzling body dances upon my shadow,

she does not interrupt the action of the self

to find one self a part of the momentary radiance

of the world if only because in this gilt autumn light

we are so many tangled breathing shapes dwelling

between air and ground, even my shadow is made

into something that holds her,

and when she chases my shadow until it dissolves

in the shadow of the mountain's life and cannot find me

under its sway, how can I not stand still

and feel her run all over me, stomping

and singing as she falls from orbit,

all the time bounded by the simple power

of what enters us, making itself felt,

bearing down on this emergent life

before it slips away.

Orchard Elegy

for Matthew Power

Heading the wrong way—north,
or circling above the orchard

with no deliberate design, I watch the geese
re-forming the simple, leaden desire

for more time. The sky, otherwise,
is prosaic,

unequivocally the end
of October; it asks to be seen

for the nothing it is. Today
you would have been alive

another year,
carrying my daughter on your shoulders

toward heaven still
to pick from highest boughs

and not let fall. I know,
the perfect continuous conditional.

Ice seals off the marsh.
Trees are only partial.

It doesn't feel right
to keep living without you.

Look how the bodies of all things
orient, then diminish—

the compulsion for home
is always light. If I close my eyes

the flight calls are audible
across the earth's surface,

and the air is redolent
of apple, child, fire, bone, you, not you.

Motherhood

Play stops at the whistle
when the striker loses her footing.
Each of us sees the alignment
and is impressed. Years from now
she could be my child out there,
throwing her body into this sport,
all of its elegant breakaway
speed and cunning footwork,
the chances it will take
to outrun the others, to surpass
the sweeper, one straight shot
past the keeper, the way
they'll lift her on their shoulders
cheering for her life. My parents
are watching too: *we hope we'll live*
long enough to see her play. Still
one to nothing. The game ends
that way. Lightening
delay. I walk home
to my daughter,
each step deliberate.

The Wood-Pile

It isn't so much order
we're after, stacking firewood
pillars at each end of the pile,
then everything between
in a crisscross pattern, pieces
freshly split and tightly fit,
wedged in silence,
my father, my daughter, and I,
we carry one, two, sometimes three
at a time, each memory
of northeast forest,
fragrant and splintered
into a form we will gradually
ruin, a slow burn
for the sole pleasure
of the body's warmth,
we build it high
until we think we've found
a stable point,
my father, my daughter, and I,
so that later we can step back
from it, admire our work,
see how it exists without
our meddling, the way
we only ever wanted
something (to lean towards,
to draw from)
that would not topple.

Latitudes of a Mother

Bird by dead bird,
someone is keeping count
of what strikes the city
without seeing its reflection
in time. Meanwhile from earth,
miles north under the flyway—
a field between silence,
the circle of us wonders what it is
to fall upward. It's a story
we've been working on. One character
queers the simple sky. One
is made to envelop history
and has no care
of the body's formality.
I am not one of them.
There go the geese.
There is the woman who held me
down with the force of wind.
There is a house with no one
who knew how to stay.
Eventually we all die my daughter
says with no feeling
walking beside me
along the creek. At four,
the magic sticks she found
in the forest can reverse
any story. You can be brought back
from the dead. *If you are dead*
we can fix you, she waves her sticks.
And what does dead mean, asks my mother
later when the sun has dropped
us into the unblinded window,
hurt or gone? It used to be
we could hide who we were,
but look at us there,
like all we have is the name

for what love makes, and
no one hasn't already
picked up the birds,
the crashed ones
who could not be fixed.

III

Northeastern Tracks

Sometimes, I don't know where to begin.
The sun is dead. The chickens were mauled.
The cattle burned. The baby in my belly
will come too late to know the woman
who raised me like a mother.
Every object in the still-life of farm
restores the sorrows that love
cannot dismantle, treading
on the iced-over swamp
of January, our bodies percussive
in the way of ghosts, each crack echoing
deep within the land's quiet hollow,
and parts of us, we can't possibly protect,
falling through. *The business of life and death*,
my friend calls it, then describes what survived
the fire. We keep walking. The silver maple
is a question of shadow.
Three sister sheep press their faces
to the slightest opening in the fence
to be touched. I take my hand out
of my glove and understand
how one spark could give this life
purpose or ravage it. We never know
the whole story. Back at the house,
we look at the tracks
we've left behind: bound, diagonal,
the escape route, the scale of a thing
pursued. I see rivers of milk.
I see the scar of barn. And yet, who
would not choose to be born? Beauty,
I'm not sure if you're the pasture
that erases my feet or the lighted sky
under which I long to be found.

Prelude to a Daughter on the Norske Trail

Not until we were adrift in forest
did I begin to feel

that you were the only thing
growing in winter,

and even then,
who could hear a distress call

as prayer? Some animal
near or far

in the understory,
impossible to know.

What does it matter
when all of this matter

is eventual elegy.
We heed the warning:

No hemlocks,
no trout.

To love a thing not yet in the world,
To stand at the edge of woods

then walk among yellow birches
with their ragged outer lives,

bowing and toppling
is to know

wonder.
Even trees feel things.

A stream still
moves.

It is like me to return
for a pile of bones,

to carry them
with a tenderness

reserved only for the living
in my hardened cold palms

under the blankest sky,
hearing a pulse. I cannot identify

its presence. To which animal
did it succumb?

Now you know something about terror.
Now you are divisible.

There is heartwood
inside the tamarack tree.

Listen for it
as you move

with the speed
of two wills.

Prospect Park in February

Past the silver linden where they buried half of you,
Icy arms overhanging and the wasted breath

Of passers-by looking inward.
Past the mucky pond

Where dogs rescue morning
From a stillness

So disarranged it hurts
To be a body, kicking

For no reason at all.
Past the baseball diamond

Where no one's on-deck,
A mother chasing the one life she made.

Northern Valleys Elsewhere

Another February, no thing
as I once knew it:

the woods still
with wanting,

snow angling toward earth,
miniature heart of yours

beating inside my
lovelorn body,

how it is
and is not

the life
I forage.

Autobiography of Winter

Form's what affirms
—JAMES MERRILL

Don't make me say what I want
of your life as I come to an end.
Here a tree, there a tree,
each one in the suspense of light.
How long I have been living
for this alone. Once, I was the field
you knew as snow and when
you fell down on me, I
was your imprint. What made you
believe your loneliness
was special. I was everywhere,
the hardened truth of time,
each spindly shadow and the stillness
none could reach. I was born
as water and when I appeared,
when I was something made
from nothing, it was only to wake
you from your own cold eye
for unannounced beauty: detail
in woods, line where sky
happened, bones of the orchard
you ate from. It was only
to hold your withinness.
To narrate recurrence.
Some days I am no more
than the silence in your hand
wanting to be held.

Family Portrait

All day the snow slanted
towards us.
We did things to feel part
of the tableau:
opened our mouths to it,
became angels, rolled a body
into falsely solid form.
We were like all the others
enduring a forecast of zeroes.
There were three of them
and one of me. And each time
I walked back up the same hill
inclined to call their names
as they floated away, the whirling
shapes of my daughters,
the shrill joy of my daughters,
sledding into the blankness
of their lives, no accident
of velocity, somewhere
my own blessed mother
lowering the curtain.

Northeast Brazil

On the bus to Salvador, a woman gives me her baby. She says she likes the sound of my voice. We are speeding through the interior. Past vivid towns we once lived in. Past blue cave lagoons and ochre-red rivers we once plunged in. We once dazzled. I see dusty children in rooms without walls. I see a broken road. A burning haven. The sun is an eye. The church is a mouth. It opens and shuts. *There are too many waterfalls*. There are diamonds inside the plateau that erodes. How uneasy it is to become a mother. I rock the baby, sing to the baby, promise the baby that when we return to the city, I will walk her into the Bay of All Saints. She will swim away from this peninsula. To the island. Beyond the country. And be free. These are imperatives with no evidence. She will miss the Carnival. We will not have danced in disguise. When the bus pulls into the station, the woman is sleeping. She has forgotten what she was meant for. I will remind her. Or forgive her. I could make a life of this.

The Cardinal

The only color in winter
is the ghost of her
through a window
looking in at us
while we do simple acts
of living: chew food,
wash dishes, recycle
news of the war
elsewhere, a mother dragged
the distance. Sometimes
I get down on my knees
to collect the crumbs
from the mouths
of my children, who
can't possibly ever know
the absence
of joy I feel. There I am
crawling under the table,
like I don't know how
to get back up and be
their mother. And there
she is, wanting a way in,
the faintest breath against glass.

Marriage Story

Just when I thought no one thing could belong
to another in this wooded winter
which was not already gone,
enveloped, somehow more faintly itself,
the mountain breathing snow
into weightless motion,
that we could glide through wanting
to pass warmth between our mouths
but never trying, or the blur where the sun
had grown cold might split
open long enough to return feeling
to our fingers so that we might cling
to it, then realize our lapse in remembering
the complications of touch,
how deeply I feared that no one
who would join me in this life
would not disappear into the blank script

of landscape—I saw the still-full
beech trees, their papery withered leaves
stirring everywhere I looked, *how*
could it be possible? and the woman
in gentle stride beside me saying *they appear*
fragile yet their hold is strong, each of us
free to love again. What does it mean
to ask good questions of this earth
in order to save it? What does it mean to leave
a marriage to save ourselves? Which of these
could offer evidence: science
or metaphor? I needed to know
why they persist
when everything else has long let go—
a strategy to reduce loss
and damage, to protect, to deter, to fade
but not to shed, not to fall off,

or to hang on defiantly
past its moment. *No one*
can say with absolute certainty why it happens.
If I were the wind circulating
through the forest I would never feel
lonely again. Even though the friction
we're accustomed to beneath our feet
is not there, we keep rerouting,
and somebody's policies might take all
of this away—each thing
held in place for us to honor,
to retain, to not disjoin
from the story
we couldn't become of us.

Desire as Snowdrift

It was my first try at love
again. We stayed in range,
a silent skate through motions
of wanting. How the forest
held still for us. How it made us
part of something darker. At first
I couldn't speak. I let things be
done to me. I thought,
this is the only body I have
left. How would it ever be
known? We stopped
where the light broke through.
Field me, I said. And the quiet
built me a house, but all the doors
were fluent in closing. How
I wanted a way in. I even begged.
But she did animal things
and I was born.
Après-ski at the brewery,
we drank Woods & Waters ale.
Later, her fingers—across the place
where my babies once lived,
the cragged ridge of scar
and stories of entrance—
strong and unremitting and
all the pleasure I could not accept.

Winter Remembrance

Sometimes   while out   for a ski
through the grove   and over the hills
behind   the old pine-shadowed house
where   my three daughters   ease
into   mid-day slumber   and grow
farther away   with each kick
and glide   under the muted blue
of sky   so serene,   I forget
        how to   remember
a time   before I was a mother.
The land   is nothing   without
this parenthesis of ice-laden trees:
if something may be   *bound,*
     it may also be   *unbound.*
There   are the loping tracks   of an animal.
There is the story   I tell   myself
of what it was   running from.

3 A.M. Sestina After the Birth

Throw away the lights, the definitions,
And say of what you see in the dark
　　—WALLACE STEVENS, "THE MAN WITH THE BLUE GUITAR"

I kept them unnamed, they were mine for a time
then taken, somewhere in the dark
near-death of their living while my hands
were tied, the lovesick mother, the hollow mother
sewn shut, a silenced thing looking for sound, a body
and its missing parts, held in a room without light.

Through the window I watched evening fall: dull light,
November rain, steel bridge over city, all of time
flowing on; how I wanted to be the verb of river, my body
stitched with the love of those two in the dark
trying to breathe, I was their mother,
emptied-out, clasping each supple shadow with both my hands.

To know them suddenly and yet to know nothing: whose fisted hands,
whose furled limbs, whose gasping breath rising into air like light,
whose mother staring at the resemblance of mother,
gone from this scene, whose tears. For the first time
I saw them. Baby B alongside me in the dark,
Baby A wired to the breathing machine of her body,

three floors below us, in the room where her body
would be saved, renamed, turned over for air. How her hands
reached for me while I hid in the dark
only to be found. And she with her sister latched to the light
of me, taking what they could, and there was no other time
I was so alive, they were living, flesh of the mother.

Then we were home, alone together, a mother
and her babies, and we were all of us hungry, our body
couldn't get enough, we lost track of time,
it was always almost morning, I prayed it would come, my hands

their lips my breasts their eyelids, the space of light
between us, rooting in a half-sleep, slipping into dark.

I won't leave out the mother on her knees crying, too, in the dark
or what I might have sung, lullaby of generous wind, if I were the mother
I thought I could be, to soothe them, to carry them into the light
as only a mother can with her one body
alone and release it all to them. Those nights my hands
pressed their mouths to take from me every sweet drop of time.

And they did. And we floated there in the dark beyond time.
Imagine the mother they made me. Full are my hands,
and those are the beams of my body. And they are rare sources of light.

Moonrise Over Mountains

After dinner, I carry my three year-old out to the front lawn deep with snow to watch the moonrise. Three degrees feels like negative, and she's only wearing a shirt because she peed her pants while I was clearing the dishes from the table. But here's the thing, I have this idea that my body alone can warm her. That if we keep walking until we've left the lamplight glow of the house where the babies are still in their highchairs, beyond the yard, across the road, and into the field, there will only be the luster of moon, in full, a deep orange orb rising gently over the eastern mountains, brightening, and just the two of us shivering there. I hold every part of her close. Any way you name it, we could compose meaning: Wolf Moon, Hunger Moon, *Moon of Life at its Height*. We are all of these things. The stars faintly form a *winding river*. Our breath floats there between us. *Everything is just so beautiful*, my child says, *I'm cold*. I take her inside: dirty plates, smell of piss, whining, etcetera. How careless to think I could be enough. Or that this could be less than everything.

First Light in Temescal Canyon

Always the coreopsis—giant tangle of yellow
along the bluff

to overrule the negative space
of you—catches my heart

off guard. Four winters gone now,
long enough to identify

what is endemic to this canyon:
black sage, red maids, stars

of gold, wishbone.
But also:

fossils, faults, fire
burning all of it.

Somehow, life continues. Language
tells us *survival depends on frequency.*

I want to be frequent to the light
falling off the jagged shoulder of Skull rock.

I want to be frequent to the sinking air
on its descent to the Earth's surface, to the Flicker,

the Junco, the Thrasher, the lover,
the daughter whose feet dance

so near to my heart, sometimes
I cannot breathe.

After all, it was you, mother
of my mother, who showed me

what love could do,
could not do. What am I

meant to grieve
while I peer inside one body

to know another,
a lineage of moving parts

I count: one hand (swaying), one hand (raised),
two eyes (unopened)—arriving the way

you left this world, precisely. *You can go
now*, I whispered in your ear

as if you needed permission.
How many mornings

walking through fog
along the north-

facing escarpment, where the trail enters
chaparral, looking for someone

to count me
among the living,

anyone to remind me I am not
so alone.

What I can't imagine
is how quickly all of this will ignite,

how I'll press the baby
against my hollowed-out figure

while ashes unspool noiselessly
all around us,

and horses gallop for their lives
in a cerement of smoke,

muscling down the canyon,
crossing the highway to reach ocean,

everything
rife and spare at once.

IV

*Give me a world, you have taken the
world I was.*
—ANNE CARSON

Song of the Phoebe

Out looping the meadow
I stop at the mark in the land
years after the wedding,
loved ones in the dark
glowing at the center,
gone now. What I wouldn't do
to have them back.
Return to that night, fail
all over again. Just to see
their faces. There is so much
that is common to this place,
you could miss it. Each time
I come and go, careful
not to agitate the phoebe
nesting in the eaves
who sings continuously
in her bundle of muck & moss.
A loner,
all she can do is utter
her own name. Imagine
only having yourself to call
home, over and over, no one
to notice your coming or going,
no one to say *where were you,
I was waiting my whole life*.

How My Children Were Made

Not with lust,
though the unsettled lover that carries my child
through woods of tapped maple trees
laid the sum of her muscular body on top of mine last night
and I wondered what could be made of that feeling,
already one hand on my belly holding the two of them warm,
deep in snow and the slow drip of sap into each pail.

We're walking with the biologist from Toulouse
whose burly husband fires up the sugar shack while their two sons
trail behind, and I stay at her side, wanting the closeness
of another mother. It's too early to know which heart
is viable, or how I will explain the singular life
I've chosen, with each step cautious not to fall on the ice-
rooted path, I hold onto anything within reach—the blunt light
of sky, her arm, the lover, my child, trunk of the hardwood—I want
to open my mouth and taste what there is.

No view of the mountains,
only a matter of time. But this is where
we would admire things like *eminence, panorama,*
perspective, or note the way our bodies are made
expansive by the intimacy of strangers who see us. What other way
do we know we are home? The science
of existence directs us to a language of outcomes. If this,
then this. I've read about the generosity
of trees, especially the *mothers,* ancient and wise, that nurture
and grieve and perceive each body
that passes through. *Silhouette, shadow.* And here we are taking
what we can for our own sweet pleasure.

At the clinic, the doctor named the risk factors,
and when it was over, praised his collection
of eggs. I was still nothing
more than a repository of longing, I was no one's passion, held
down by other forces. And months later, I watched the film

of my uterus on the screen—all I had to do
was lie there while two embryos were released
into the dark of me
until the lights went out, and I was infinitely alone,
only the nurse's hand to hold.

What part of this
is luck? What part of luck
contains happiness? What part
of happiness is the fact of our interdependence?
Of desire is science. Of taste is feeling. Of instinct
is love. Of child is poetry.
There's no need to apologize for the clouds.
Do you want to discuss reduction? the doctor asked me.
And to think of the frailty of trees
when other trees are removed. The sentience
of the forest, alive yet mute.
That I could choose to eliminate one
and keep the other. That something was taking form
at the boiling point, and all I could do
was open my mouth to the pure amber light echoing
from the place where the mountains
should have been, sticky and solicitous and eager.

Depth of Field

There's a photograph of me stopped
on the trail that edges Drake's Bay

pointing a camera at Chimney Rock,
the eastern spur of headlands.

Behind me is a woman
I will stop loving,

a pier broken
with time,

a lifeboat station,
the gleam of Pacific,

so much that is not possible
if only I would turn around.

But I've spotted the colony
of northern elephant seals

that returns to this rookery
every winter, hauled out

on the southwest end of the beach,
their colossal bodies warring

and hitching, a display so dramatic,
I don't read the signs.

Through one lens
everything erodes:

this ridge of rugged land,
her body, my trust.

Do not climb cliffs.
Do not trample plants.

The fragility of it all
is ours.

Through another lens:
a mother

coming to shore alone,
the echo of her

streamlined body traveling
up from the cove below,

where embattled bulls
roar and trumpet for dominion.

My eye follows
the wake of tufted puffins

at play, a contrast to
the unruly harem.

But I am seeing all of this
from the future,

not knowing you
will want to be born.

Tonight, while you sleep in the next room,
I watch footage of a seal

giving birth in that same spot,
dragging the weight of herself

a long way until the pup finally releases,
skua gulls circling above,

then go to find you,
place my hand on your chest in the dark

to make sure you're still
here.

You are—
a rising and falling heart—

what I must have been looking for
all along,

where the estuary feeds the bay,
where ships continue to wreck.

Weather of Someplace

I wanted a body of water to live near. To live by the body. To get inside the body of another woman and swallow there. To float like a body in the found water of love. To know myself there. Now, miles from any line of coast. Rain all day in the valley. Mountain with fog and winding roads blank. Eye on the sky narrates a system of pressure from the Cape to the Great Lakes, where a friend writes *hoping I'll continue to feel nothing,* and we are between. The landlock of one kind of presence. The incision to remove what doesn't live. And *what does the brain matter compared with the heart?* Three daughters keep watching their feet keep disappearing, their reflections as earth telling sky to persevere. What would the tree say to the tree that feels pain? Things grow inside of us without our permission. Love has no say. We are only humans marveling at the sudden turning of chokecherry. With every utterance I know a word hurts for its beauty. There's too much to not love. Those are tears on my face though I prefer to describe cloud-spill, spindrift, the prism after storm. I'll tell you what's missing from my life. You and you and you. Look me up sometime. Hold my mouth near yours but never speak of it. Every time I go home, home has a way of being elsewhere.

First Scan of Twins

Sometimes the merlins that roost at the top
of our only living pine tree

work as a pair
to bring down songbirds in surprise attacks.

One swoops up from below while
One takes advantage of the confusion.

In those moments, I'm awed
by the ferocity

of something so small to survive.
First the silent scan,

unseen by the human
eye, then the acceleration of wing-

beats, continuous and rhapsodic.
First, a blaring cackle

punctuates the suspended silence,
then the plaintive calls of each one

overtaken. Nothing unbeautiful
in loss escapes us.

And when winter returned in April,
only my mother could understand

I wasn't expecting it.
I wept. I threw up

in the backyard kicking the soccer ball
with my daughter. And when we found a single,

blue-streaked feather in the drift, all I could hear
were the echoes of so many pieces

of song falling
with the tenderness of new snow.

Garden Prayer

Breaking ground, your body is all
I think about. In the sky,

kestrels hovering, the alarm
of swallows, a red-winged flash,

everything somehow coming
alive though you are dead.

It doesn't feel right. Gnarled
roots of last summer, I pull

with force, a tangle
of artichoke, surprise of April

worms, stalky remnants,
the promise of so much

broken and specific. You
are under my feet, earth-

bound, *at peace*, says the priest.
Also, you are the zephyr

that passes through the birch copse
and over my shadow. How

can I possibly accept this bright world
being given to me so effusively

without you? What faith there is
in repetition: I dig,

fill the wheelbarrow, empty it
in the woods, fill, empty.

There is no choice
but to accept the precise lives

of budding trees, vociferous robins
and phoebes, their earthly song,

I listen for you. *Pain
goes away*, says the priest. *Happiness*

*comes back. That's the difference.
Come back,*

I want to say to you. *Come back,*
I want to say to happiness.

The soil is warm
again. I press the seeds of pole beans

into new ground and it is like this,
the stubborn coherence of living matter,

my own useless power
to revive you.

Hymn of the Trees

life is the swaying up and the swaying down
of great forest branches and clinging to life . . .
        —HD

There we are on the floor
of a rented apartment in the East Village,
twenty-something, our whole lives impossibly
ahead of us.

                        But I keep trying
                        to start this poem with the box
                        that held your body years later:
                        perfectly square, solid, latched
                        shut.

Not with the way I moved my hands
under your shirt to feel the constellation
of marks on your back, then
down your pants to pull you onto me
with every fear I might actually enjoy
the weight of a man. No,

                        that is not a memory worthy
                        of the beauty
                        this poem wants to begin with,
                        the one I don't own, the one
                        your widow described of marigolds,
                        red and yellow, draped over you,
                        an illumination raised on a pyre in Kampala,
                        attendants caring for your body until
                        it turned to ash.

Instead, I prefer the hard
concrete floor where your body is on top
of mine, reeking of tobacco and week-old sweat,
all a mess of rough-skinned hands,

fitful lips, and the tongue that kept pushing
through, breathless with something more like hunger
than love, though I loved and
did not love the way I became a stranger
to the city of cluttered half-windows
showing us to the world, its bitter warnings
of horn, siren, merriment from the avenue
below, stupid drunken bodies in aimless
motion. It wasn't even that pleasurable—
the heavy breath and bones of you passed out
on me, and my own callow surrender,
taking what I could, stuck there, awake
with no chance of shutting my body
off; how I craved more, smoke
from the alley, greasy meat
off the restaurant's griddle exhaust
rising, a stale taste in my mouth.

        We were so alive then.
        Let me start over.
        It's April on the mountain,
        we're walking under the hole of sky
        to find the perfect place to bury you—a circle
        of birches just off Route 125.
        My feet keep sinking into sodden ground,
        warm enough now to open
        to put you inside.

Remember the linden
we climbed bough by bough
that midnight in November
and put our mouths together for heat,
swaying at the very top? Could it be true
the trees feel pain? How
do we climb down from that tree,

bough by bough, to learn
the body doesn't last?

How many hours
does it take for you to burn bright
then extinguish? I hardly slept
for days, wondering why it was my life
that went on. I returned
to the mountain, circled you, got down
on my knees to touch the earth of you
now beneath me: root, rhizome, bark—you
are in every part of it, in the wildness
of the boughs, and you are nowhere:
ashes, dust, dirt.

Pain is a gift, someone says. I look for it.
New York has just turned off its lights for song-
birds. I didn't let you inside me that night
though now I'm not sure
what I couldn't permit myself to want
which wouldn't eventually become enumerated
as loss. I listen for it. Here in the darkness
is the salvage of your limbs.
I need to get out from under you.

First Trimester in Joshua Tree

If you walk far enough into the low desert in one direction, just off Highway 62 along the northern boundary of the park, winding up three hundred feet around the rocky ridgetop then descending steeply into the canyon where the San Andreas fault has shaped a secret, you arrive, finally, at the oasis of forty-nine fan palms where I begin to feel you quickening, I swallow the heat of morning, I rest under their canopy and take note of what thrives: 1) The spiny, cylindrical red barrel cactus, planted by miners to mark our path to the source of water—how our needs remain the same; 2) A sea of fragrant brittlebush clusters, their shallow taproots waiting for rainfall then opening umbrellas of brilliant yellow—but solitary; 3) The creosote bush, rising from nothing, monarch of the land; 4) You, from crown to rump the size of a clenched fist opening. At first, I couldn't understand the desert. I took note: brown, barren, dusty. Then: cloudless, oceanic. And with every step in my fortieth year, I imagined I was steering us home, while military planes circled overhead, eyeing their rescue. I took note: my body has never been more beautiful than now, and no one is here to witness what it can do. Where did I go wrong? Though I know you float inside me why on earth do I feel something is missing? Later, moonlight on the boulders outside the cabin and we glow—the whole of us.

Dreamscape After the Shooting

First I would shut off the murder of crows rasping in the neighbor's maple tree: unruly chorus of the loneliness I will hide from my children as long as it takes.

Then I would land the low-flying plane that just misses the arms of the spruce-lined road to nowhere: a failed embrace, the suspense of impact.

If I am the one looking up from the earth at the zero of sky, who would find me burying wind into the scenery then running for my life on soundless legs: no one.

When the rains come again, each of us stands at the window watching the grave of this country deepen: not each of us drowns.

Stay with me. What I see could happen to anyone we resemble.

A man is pointing his body at objects in the mirror, only the reflection is the world shot through: with pain.

There are the women strewn in the field, in close range: How can I possibly carry their suffering home with me?

Vernal Heart

The way the dog holds the treefrog in his mouth so tenderly,
He means to almost love it as he conquers it.

Spring comes to the earth revolving only to be warmed,
And the captor is unaware of the home

He has built upon a graveyard of quick rivers.
To be able to walk towards anyone

is to say *I want you to want me beside you*,
The mud-encumbered song of feet,

The begging lisp of grasses in the light that shimmers,
Oh to understand that love is a thing of will,

When the gods put back the birds that merge in the sky,
And the discarnate shadows dance aimlessly—never to pine.

Anatomy of a Canyon

I.
It isn't the overlook I remember,
or what it promised—city

cut through with boulevards
coursing west, the hollow gulf

of Lower canyon below, or
on a clear day, the shimmering

Pacific ocean—
but the way we rose

steadily
up the fire road that turned

to a single bony track
through a chaparral-covered slope

into the obscurity of fog
with only the miracle

of our own weary bodies
to imagine the view.

II.
Ten years to find the center
of Los Angeles,

twenty weeks for a glimpse
of the life I'd assembled

at forty, a complicated transfer
from lab to womb, now

at the point of being
something from nothing,

and still anything could happen.
Look how the curve of spine aligns.

Look at the map
of outflow tracts,

those four chambers, tiny
reservoirs muddled

and magnified.
Lean in

to count the beats per minute,
though we know the evolution

of landforms
consists of irregularity.

This is a home
along the Flyway. Look

how the doctor traces the length of her,
the way we walk this mountain

wanting a way to trust the earth.
Look: detail of lips,

shape of the cerebellum.
She's quite the dancer.

Look how she begins
a pirouette.

III.
Later, at the nature center,
we kneel among the bones

and skins of mammals,
preserved with such explicit care:

yellow eyes of the mounted lynx,
bristly tail of the coyote.

I hand over the skull of a gopher
to the son of my friend,

so that he might feel
we have something in common.

And when we stop at Heavenly Pond
on our way out of the canyon,

just another human-
made anomaly, slider turtles basking

each one on the back of another
for warmth, he throws a stone

at the duo of drifting Wood ducks.
What sinks or does not sink

is not apparent.
All that time we went looking

for something to resemble real life,
something to take care of,

to pass between us, to name, god
that it would keep thriving,

that it wouldn't have been too much
beauty at once—

we would have given our lives
for one impetuous look

at the thing inside of us,
clearer by the moment.

Phenology of Home

And when my child
is asleep in the next room,
having read the book about the bear
who won't awaken from winter,
and the woman puts her mouth
to my fingers, clavicle, shoulders, loneliest
part of my back (as the wife I once loved
called it), one reason to not
unmarry, though we did,
I don't understand how
to make space for anyone
to take care of my body. By Spring,
she will be gone. The air will be thick
with cows calving in the eye
of storms. With relief,
with longing. The red-winged
blackbird will have flown back.
I will stand with my child
in a field of mud
until we can't feel our feet
and know there's nowhere
to move but towards each other.
There's no one else I can love
as well. And those hills, the first yellow
blaze of weeds we call flowers, which
eventually become the silvery stars we breathe
away, and unlike so few things
do not require our attendance
to flourish.

Spring

After the rain, worms
are carried in small palms *to safety*
into the grave of the garden
that will need them
as they need it. We call this
belonging. At night
when I am alone again,
I think of their bodies slithering,
how easily they go from less
to more to less, as if swallowing
their own hearts. Something
in my throat is caught.
I can't make the word for devotion
go away—and how close
it is to crush. There are worms
everywhere. There are children
who might never look up
to see me in pieces.
I sleep coiled without touch.

First of March

For a while we believe the iced-in world
is the real one. There is no reason
to come out from it. The fire warms
us, so does volcanic wine, and soup
made from the bones of the animal
down the road. *Is it cow or pig?* my daughter
asks, and all I feel is guilt. The plow
comes and goes, the only sign of human
contact. I miss friends in the city
I once called home. I miss the West,
ripples of heat in the desert, the chair
at the pool at the lodge in Palm Springs
where I floated on my back for days
that March of two deaths, thorny
bougainvillea crawling pink on every wall.
How did I get here from there? Down the hall,
my father combs my daughter's hair.
My mother reads a rhyming book
to the babies, and surely their fingers
try to touch each page. The days
repeat. The windows are blank.
We wake, we eat, we sleep. What more
from this life am I permitted to want
while the survival of others depends
on me alone? Then everything melts:
snowbank, spruce, garden grave-
yard, ghost-berry. A wind blows
the swing. It is lighter longer. And as if
there's nothing to mourn, my daughter jumps
maniacally in the driveway puddle,
some song in her head from the future.

Half-Life in Spring

Wonder—is not precisely Knowing
And not precisely Knowing not—
    —EMILY DICKINSON

This same day in March you die again on me every year.
        It should be the opposite
of dying but what would we name it? The springing out
        from the body that won't wake, the pressure
to look at what shines, to bring it inside with us, inside
        of us, lay it down in a winter room, the shining
body where a memory needs me to live.

        Snow underfoot and the florid mud-song of birds
that usher me out. The geese again. The bright numb pain
        of sun throwing itself over every expired thing of this earth
unmoved for months, to stun the heart. If only
        I could make myself love it the way it loves me.

Animals know how. Out from the burrowing
        only to give in. Take the duo of ladybugs
my daughter names after her sisters, fluttering like mad,
        dead by morning. Or the raccoon split quick
down the tired middle, and how we veered.

        The die-off of one thing to make space
for another. *No music if no silence.* But what
        is a landscape when no one can hear it
sing? Is death color or shade? When I retreat
        who will turn the image of my body
into a word that is not the noun of stillness?

Bloom, branch, root. Such simple ways
        to understand betweenness. In *miraculum*
is the object of wonder. In sky
        is the low-flying flock that startles. In view
is the miracle of these daughters you'll never hold,
        and the melting world I'm expected to praise.

Trees are seldom fooled by a false start. They *race*
            to grab light, and, like us, insist on loving
what keeps leaving. Loyalty is sporadic.
            Feelings are the weather. Lately, I am the wind
poised to reverse, and I am the peace after wind.
            But what are you
of this splendiferous earth
            and so far gone?

Everywhere underground
            the quarrel of wakeful things. Elsewhere:
people showing off their terrible ebullience. I should
            be kinder, I should say *hello* and *goodbye,* but I want
none of it today, or tomorrow.

            If translation is an act of retrieval,
it is cruel, what language would have us believe.
            If I tell the story of you enough times,
will you appear? This morning
            someone's cat left me the heart of a mouse
at my front door. Tell me where in this world
            can I not find you.

And there you are in the face of my daughter,
            in the soft line of her cheek, glint of her eye, name I whisper
calling me out
            to bask in the light of the sun's numinous body:
a study in hope,
            as diffuse as our lives can bear it,
can bloom it. I lived for so long uprooted while all along
            the tree was a system of transport, the bare-
bone deceit of green.

You were always praying to be reborn.
Look at my daughter hanging from that one bending branch
        with the breath of your wings, and her animal reckoning:
conciliatory, enraptured, unknowing.
        Life, for her, can only be literal, so when I tell her *you will die*

of happiness, of course I mean live, not die.
        Live, not diminish
from the pain of too much infinite beauty. How many ways can I remember
        you? *Touch with your eyes* I tell her, marvel at the thing
as if you were never coming back
        again. Let it shine on you.

Notes

The opening epigraph of this book is from Rainer Maria Rilke's *Book of Hours*.

The epigraph to "June Landscape with Child" is from Paul Celan's "Great, Glowing Vault" translated from German by Pierre Joris in *Breathturn*: Die Welt is fort, ich muss dich tragen.

The title "Body Electric" is borrowed from Walt Whitman's "I Sing the Body Electric."

"Mornings at the Lake" quotes from Henry David Thoreau's *Walden*.

The epigraph to II is from Virginia Woolf's *To the Lighthouse*.

The epigraph to "LA Translations" is from William Butler Yeats' poem, "Nineteen Hundred and Nineteen."

"Orca Elegy" draws from the Orca named *Talequah*, a word in Cherokee legend that means *two is enough*, or *just two*. The poem culls from various news articles documenting the moment, and references Snell's window.

The title of "The Life of Shadows" is borrowed from David Abram's *Becoming Animal: An Earthly Cosmology*. Part I is an erasure poem based on an excerpt from this book; Part II is an alternate response, or rather, a shadow version.

"Orchard Elegy" quotes from Robert Frost's poem "After Apple-Picking."

The epigraph to "Autobiography of Winter" is from James Merrill's poem "The Thousand and Second Night."

"Northeast Brazil" quotes from Elizabeth Bishop's poem "Questions of Travel."

"Marriage Story" references the phenomenon marcescence.

The epigraph to IV is from Anne Carson's poem "O Small Sad Ecstasy of Love."

"Weather of Someplace" quotes from Virginia Woolf's *Mrs. Dalloway*.

The epigraph to "Hymn of Trees" is from HD's novel *Asphodel*.

"Vernal Heat" is a term borrowed from Robert Frost's "Two Tramps in Mud Time."

The epigraphs "3 A.M. Sestina After the Birth" is from Wallace Stevens' poem "The Man with the Blue Guitar."

The epigraph to "Half-Life" *in Spring* is from Emily Dickinson's poem #1331. The lines "trees are seldom fooled by a false start" and "race to grab light" were borrowed from Bernd Heinrich's *Winter World*.

About the Lexi Rudnitsky Editor's Choice Award

The Lexi Rudnitsky Editor's Choice Award is given annually to a poetry collection by a writer who has published at least once previous book of poems. Along with the Lexi Rudnitsky First Book Prize in Poetry, it is a collaboration of Persea Books and the Lexi Rudnitsky Poetry Project. Entry guidelines for both awards are available on Persea's website (www.perseabooks.com).

Lexi Rudnitsky (1972–2005) grew up outside of Boston, and studied at Brown University and Columbia University. Her own poems exhibit both a playful love of language and a fierce conscience. Her writing appeared in *The Antioch Review, Columbia: A Journal of Literature and Art, The Nation, The New Yorker, The Paris Review, Pequod,* and *The Western Humanities Review*. In 2004, she won the Milton Kessler Memorial Prize for Poetry from *Harpur Palate*.

Lexi died suddenly in 2005, just months after the birth of her first child and the acceptance for publication of her first book of poems, *A Doorless Knocking into Night* (MidList Press, 2006). The Lexi Rudnitsky book prizes were created to memorialize her by promoting the type of poet and poetry in which she so spiritedly believed.

Previous winners of the Lexi Rudnitsky Editor's Choice Award

2021   Sarah Carson, *How to Baptize a Child in Flint, Michigan*

2020   Christopher Salerno, *The Man Grave*

2019   Enid Shomer, *Shoreless*

2018   Cameron Awkward-Rich, *Dispatch*

2017   Gary Young, *That's What I Thought*

2016   Heather Derr-Smith, *Thrust*

2015   Shane McCrae *The Animal Too Big to Kill*

2014   Caki Wilkinson, *The Wynona Stone Poems*

2013   Michael White, *Vermeer in Hell*

2012   Mitchell L. H. Douglas, *blak**al-f bet*\

2011   Amy Newman, *Dear Editor*